CW01666978

GALE
CENGAGE Learning

Novels for Students, Volume 31

Project Editor: Sara Constantakis Rights Acquisition and Management: Jennifer Altschul, Margaret Chamberlain-Gaston, Leitha Etheridge-Sims, Kelly Quin Composition: Evi Abou-El-Seoud Manufacturing: Drew Kalasky

Imaging: John Watkins

Product Design: Pamela A. E. Galbreath, Jennifer Wahi Content Conversion: Katrina Coach Product Manager: Meggin Condino

For product information and technology assistance, contact us at **Gale Customer Support, 1-800-877-4253.**
For permission to use material from this text or product, submit all requests online at **www.cengage.com/permissions.**
Further permissions questions can be emailed to **permissionrequest@cengage.com** While every effort has been made to ensure the reliability of the information presented in this publication, Gale, a part of Cengage Learning, does not guarantee the accuracy of the data contained herein. Gale accepts no payment for listing; and inclusion in the publication of any organization, agency, institution, publication, service, or individual does not imply endorsement of the editors or publisher. Errors brought to the attention of the publisher and verified to the satisfaction of the publisher will be corrected in future editions.

Gale
27500 Drake Rd.
Farmington Hills, MI, 48331-3535

ISBN-13: 978-1-4144-4169-6
ISBN-10: 1-4144-4169-X
ISSN 1094-3552

This title is also available as an e-book.
ISBN-13: 978-1-4144-4947-0

ISBN-10: 1-4144-4947-X
Contact your Gale, a part of Cengage Learning sales representative for ordering information.

Printed in the United States of America
1 2 3 4 5 6 7 14 13 12 11 10

Dune

Frank Herbert 1965

Introduction

Dune, published in 1965, helped transform the genre of science fiction from one of adolescent adventure to one of exploration of ideas. It was an unprecedented success in mainstream culture, becoming the first piece of genre science fiction to appear on the *New York Times* best-seller list. The importance of *Dune* in Herbert's career was paramount, ensuring his financial success, but also dooming him (and his son Brian Herbert) to a lifetime of writing sequels, since no other project could match its popularity. *Dune* has become the source of many media projects, including comic books, a feature film, a television miniseries, and a proposed new film series. *Dune*'s influence has spread even further, becoming the inspiration for such media projects as *Star Wars*.

Created in the 1960s, *Dune* bears the marks of the counterculture of that time in its concern for ecology. It also reflects the counterculture's distrust of authority and power in its portrayal of corrupt and manipulative institutions such as the Bene Gesserit, the CHOAM corporation, and the Spacing Guild that rule its fictive world. It also shares the optimism of the 1960s that human powers of imagination and perception could transcend and displace materialistic culture. However, *Dune* is, above all, an exploration of the role of religion and quasi-religious forces in human culture in the wake of the fascist hero cults of the 1920s and 1930s.

Author Biography

Herbert was born on October 8, 1920, in Tacoma, Washington. After a brief service in the army during World War II, he attended the University of Washington, but he did not obtain a degree because he refused to take required courses that he considered personally uninteresting and unnecessary. This marked the independence of thought that dominated his adult life. He took highly original viewpoints to arrive at highly creative solutions in his writing, but at the same time he was prone to imagine that his expertise extended to many areas in which he had no formal training. This led him to accept many pseudoscientific ideas in his own thought as well as exploring them in his writing; for instance, he believed that human can be stored in genetic material. Unusually for a science fiction author, he rejected the scientific method in favor of more holistic approaches to knowledge, whose results are, to say the least, unverifiable.

Herbert worked as a journalist in the Pacific Northwest throughout the 1950s and 1960s, eventually becoming an editor at the *San Francisco Examiner*. At the same time, he occasionally published short stories in the science fiction pulp magazines, and in 1955 he published his first novel, known variously as *Under Pressure* or *The Dragon in the Sea*. This novel takes place during a future war between the United States and the Soviet Union and concerns a psychologist evaluating the effects of combat stress on the crew of an American nuclear submarine assigned to steal oil from the Soviet-occupied Persian Gulf. The theme of scientific psychological evaluation is typical of Herbert's work.

Herbert took six years to write his next novel, *Dune*, which grew out of his convergent interests in religion, the psychology of totalitarianism, and ecology. It was serialized in *Analog* magazine between 1963 and 1965 and published in book form in 1965. It immediately won the two most prestigious awards in science fiction, the Nebula, awarded by the Science Fiction Writers of America, and the Hugo, awarded by the attendees of the annual World Science Fiction Convention. It is generally considered to be, if not the greatest science fiction novel ever written, certainly the first to attain a new level of literary achievement within the genre. With brisk book sales and the sale of film rights to the book in 1971, Herbert retired from journalism to write and lecture full time. Though he produced many independent projects, his most successful literary work was a series of five sequels to *Dune*, completed before his death from pancreatic cancer in Madison, Wisconsin, on February 11, 1986. His son Brian Herbert has written a biography of his father and several more novels continuing and expanding the story related to *Dune* based on his father's notes.

Plot Summary

The text of *Dune* is divided into three books of unnumbered chapters. Each chapter is headed by an epigraph that is a quotation, not from an existing literary work but from a pseudoscholarly work attributed to Princess Irulan, whom the reader learns only at the very end of the novel becomes Paul's wife. The various works named are supposedly historical treatises concerning her husband's early career that she wrote some time after the conclusion of the novel. Read retrospectively, these pseudoquotations reveal important points of the story that occur either in the chapter they head or in a later chapter. This violates a basic principle of ordinary storytelling: it gives away key elements of the plot. In a way, Irulan allows the reader to share in Paul's prophetic ability and see glimpses of what will happen later in the narrative.

Dune

The first several chapters are devoted as much to the exposition of the story's world as to traditional plot elements. The civilization of *Dune* spans the galaxy and is approximately ten thousand years old (how far in the future it might be from the present is never revealed). This Imperium took on its present form in response to the "Butlerian Jihad." This conflict is never clearly discussed, but it is hinted that it was a crisis in which intelligent computers attempted to exterminate or enslave the human race. Since that time, all computers have been forbidden. Perhaps as a result, there has been little technological advance since that time. Instead, various human potentials have been developed to ever greater heights of perfection. Several institutions based on human abilities rule the galaxy in concert with more traditional power structures. The central source of political power is the Combine Honnete Ober Advancer Mercantiles (CHOAM), a joint-stock corporation whose stockholders are granted absolute rule over entire planets in proportion to their stock. The expression of this rule is feudal: the chairman calls himself emperor, the other stockholders dukes and barons. Each member maintains a large military establishment that is used for protection in feuds with other magnates (under the code of *kanly*, or vendetta) and protection from the power of the emperor. The Great Houses are organized into the *Landsraat*, or parliament. Together their military power is only about equal to the emperor's since he controls the Sardaukar, a large force of soldiers whose superhuman military skill make them nearly invincible. Each Great House also has a cache of nuclear weapons (the "family atomics") that may only be used if the legal functioning of the power structure is violated. Another vital component of civilization is the *mentats*, men whose minds are trained to function as computers. Without their aid, controlling civilization on a galactic scale would be impossible, although as a class they have no independent access to power apart from the nobles they serve.

Media Adaptations

- The first film adaptation of *Dune* was made in 1984 and was directed by David Lynch.
- In 2001, *Dune* was adapted as a miniseries on the Science Fiction Channel of American cable television in three two-hour-long installments, directed by John Harrison. This version is sometimes known as *Frank Herbert's Dune*.
- In 2008, it was announced that Peter Berg would begin directing a new film adaptation of *Dune*; this version is scheduled for release in 2010.
- Several video games have been based on *Dune*: *Dune* (1992; based

on graphics from the 1984 film), *Dune II* (1992), *Dune 2000* (1998), *Emperor: Battle for Dune* (2001), and *Frank Herbert's Dune* (2001; based on graphics from the 2001 miniseries).

The rule of the Great Houses, however, extends only across the surface of planets. The Spacing Guild has complete control of all spacecraft (even weather and communications satellites can be put into orbit only with their approval). Beyond this, they have a monopoly on travel between star systems (and their final authority is to withhold this service from a Great House that might pose a challenge to them). In the absence of computers, Guild ships are guided though hyperspace by navigators who can see into the future because they take massive doses of a drug known as spice. This spice (the source of wealth of the CHOAM) is a natural product of a single planet, Arrakis (Arabic for "the dancer"). It is generally referred to as the "geriatric spice," since it is taken in lower doses by all aristocrats who can afford it for the purpose of extending life. Another powerful group is the Bene Gesserit Sisterhood (Latin for "she will have performed well"). Just as mentats and navigators are only males, the Bene Gesserit is a purely female institution. Disciplined according to a system of physical and psychological training derived from the martial arts, Zen, and yoga, the Bene Gesserits use the water of life, a spice-poison that uses the biochemistry of their own bodies to metabolize into a drug that induces a higher state of consciousness. The Reverend Mothers who have performed this rite are able to perceive the world around them absolutely (for instance, they are called truthsayers, since they can detect from the smallest telltale sign whether someone is lying) and can also see into human consciousness as a whole. The role of the Bene Gesserit in society seems to be to provide wives and concubines to the Great Houses, and they often educate daughters of the nobility. In short, Herbert presents the human civilization of the future as a finely balanced system in a state of homeostasis (constantly staying the same). However, it is a frozen system, not a dynamic one in constantly rebalanced change, and therefore it will tend to break if pressure is applied.

Dune opens with a scene in which Paul Atreides, the son of Duke Leto and his Bene Gesserit concubine Jessica, is being tested by the Reverend Mother Gaius Helen Mohaim. The test consists of having a poison dart (the *gom jabar*) held to his throat with the threat that it will instantly kill him if he removes his hand from a box that seems to be destroying his appendage in an excruciatingly painful way. When he passes the test and realizes that the pain was an illusion, Paul is told that his experience reveals that he is a human being, able to govern his response to pain and fear with reason, rather than an animal. Over the course of the first book of *Dune*, Herbert reveals that in accordance with the Bene Gesserit breeding program, Paul was meant to have been a girl (Bene

Gesserits can control the sex of their children), but out of love for the Duke, his mother Jessica bore a son in defiance of the orders of her superiors. Paul, in addition to being the heir of a duke, has been trained as a mentat by his father's mentat Thifur Hawat. He was also trained by his mother as a Bene Gesserit, although training a man in this fashion is forbidden. Paul has also been taught fencing by Gurney Halleck, the most loyal of his father's military retainers.

Paul's family is being led into a trap. Arrakis, the planet that is the sole source of geriatric spice, has been controlled for many decades by the Baron Harkonnen, an ancestral rival to the house of Atreides. Supposedly, the Emperor has removed him from control of this huge source of income on the grounds of mismanagement. The planet will instead be given to Duke Leto, who is universally admired by members of the Landsraat for his uprightness and honor. The duke is well aware, however, that this is most likely a plot to destroy him. The second chapter reveals every detail of this scheme in a staff meeting between the Baron Harkonnen, his nephew and chosen heir Feyd-Rautha, and his sadistic mentat Piter de Vries. Once the duke is established in his new holding, the baron will invade the planet in a surprise attack. Although his forces could probably be defeated by the superior training and valor of the Atreides military, the Harkonnens will be supported by sixty thousand Sardaukar from the Emperor's guard, the greatest soldiers in the galaxy.

The plot is duly carried out within a few days of Duke Leto taking possession of Arrakis, and although the matter might seem quite straightforward given the element of surprise and the overwhelming military force used, the nearly two hundred pages of the first book are used to spin out the elaborately Byzantine plot of the Harkonnens. Ruses and deceptions are used at every turn to feed the suspicions of the leaders of the House Atreides about each other. The Harkonnen plot succeeds in effecting the military defeat of the Atreides forces (they are virtually annihilated) and in killing the Duke. Baron Harkonnen believes that he has also killed Paul, the heir, and his mother Jessica, by forcing them to fly an ornithopter into a sandstorm, but in fact they survive, aided by the Imperial planetologist Pardot Keynes, whose mother was a Fremen, a member of the mysterious native population of Arrakis. Kynes is secretly Liet, the leader of the Fremen. He guarantees that the Fremen will protect the fugitive nobles.

During their escape, Paul reveals to his mother a prophetic vision of the future that he has had. He authenticates this vision by telling her that she is pregnant with a daughter, Alia (which only she knew), and with the revelation that she is the Baron Harkonnen's daughter, a fact that she has denied as unthinkable but that she now must accept based on family resemblance. She suggests that he is the Kwisatz Haderach, the male Bene Gesserit bred from thousands of years of eugenics experiments by the sisterhood; if Jessica had obeyed her Bene Gesserit orders and borne a girl, that girl would later have been the Kwisatz Haderach's mother. However, Paul tells his mother, "Put that out of your mind. I'm something unexpected." Paul does not precisely have the power to see into the future but rather to see all of the possible futures and take actions that make certain possibilities more likely. He sees two main pathways to the future, one in which he enigmatically confronts Baron Harkonnen, and another in which he unleashes a jihad, a holy war, across the galaxy to serve the purpose of remixing isolated human gene pools, but at the cost of billions of deaths. He fears pursuing either possibility.

Muad'Dib

Liet-Kynes also escapes from the Harkonnen forces, but he dies in the open desert. During his death agony he has a vision in which he obliquely reviews the ecology of Arrakis with the ghost of his father. The elder Kynes gained control of the Fremen by promising to turn Arrakis into a fertile paradise. Alluding to information that is scattered throughout the novel, Kynes realized that there was no shortage of water on Arrakis. The whole planet was a desert because its water had been trapped by an alien life form that had long ago been introduced there. This is the sandworm, referred to as the Maker or Shai-hulud by the Fremen. It is an enormous creature hundreds of meters long that swims through sand. Kynes discovered that it has a complicated natural history. The first stage of its existence is as a "little maker," a microscopic creature with both plant-like and animal-like properties that lives in the sand and sequesters any available water in cysts. Because this life was alien, it had no natural predator and so ran wild, trapping nearly all the water on the planet. The spice is a by-product of its life cycle in the desert sands. The next stage is the larva or sand-trout, a small animal that lives in the sand, feeding on the microbial form. These eventually pupate into full sandworms. Kynes devised a plan to build up green areas in the desert with water taken from the atmosphere and protected from the little makers by plants that are poisonous to them. Of course, only selected areas could be reforested or else the spice-making ecology would die out. The Fremen have been secretly carrying out this plan for several decades.

Among the Fremen, Paul and Jessica are protected by their assimilation to roles in religious mythology that the Bene Gesserit sowed among the Fremen thousands of years before through the Missonaria Protectiva. Paul is recognized as Lisan al-Gaib, the promised messiah. He uses his authority over the Fremen to lead them in a guerilla war against the Harkonnen occupying forces. He utilizes the potential of what his father called "desert power." Not only are the Fremen the greatest warriors in the galaxy thanks to the harshness of their living conditions and able to utilize the resources of the desert (such as the sandworms) for warfare, but their ultimate power is the control of the spice. Using the logical insight of his mentat training, Paul quickly deduces, "The Fremen [are] paying the Guild for privacy, paying in a coin that's freely available to anyone with desert power—spice." With their unlimited access to spice, the Fremen are able to bribe the Spacing Guild into ignoring their ecological work in the deep desert and also into denying intelligence to the Harkonnen military forces. The baron, however, cannot see the potential of the Fremen and discounts them as "rabble" He blinds himself to his greatest danger because of his arrogant, prejudiced assumptions. He pursues a course of harshly oppressing Arrakis using his nephew Glossu, so that he can later put his favored nephew Feyd-Rautha in power as a beloved savior. His ultimate aim is to position Feyd-Rautha as successor to the emperor. The baron attempts to build his nephew Feyd up to superhuman stature by making him a popular gladiator. The Bene Gesserit nevertheless do not wish to lose his lineage from their breeding program and so arrange for one of their agents, the Countess Fenring, to seduce Feyd-Rautha.

Paul and Jessica are taken in by Stilgar, the Fremen leader of Sietch Tabr. There Paul meets Chani, the daughter of Liet-Kynes and takes her as his concubine. During the fighting, Paul and the Fremen adopt many terrorist tactics, such as kamikaze attacks on troop transports that exchange the life of one pilot for the lives of hundreds of the enemy. His followers become known as Death Commandos. Jessica becomes the Reverend Mother (high priestess) of the Sietch in a ceremony in which she drinks a poison created by drowning a young sandworm. She is able to consciously control the biochemistry of her body to metabolize it into an intoxicant that is shared out among the community as a sacrament. This process calls her unborn daughter Alia to consciousness, with the result that she is able to think and speak in an adult fashion shortly after birth. Jessica also gains access to the memories of all the Fremen Reverend Mothers in the chain of succession before her.

The Prophet

Thifur Hawat has agreed to work for the Baron Harkonnen as his mentat chief of staff because he realizes that the Atreides's main enemy has been the emperor, and serving the Harkonnens puts him in the best position to directly attack the throne. Hawat reveals to the baron what the Atreides learned about the Fremen and convinces him that they should be cultivated as allies to produce a fighting force superior to the Sardaukar. He has also deduced that the reason the emperor destroyed Duke Leto was that the military proficiency of the Atreides armed forces was approaching that of the Sardaukar. The baron imagines that this new scheme of cultivating the Fremen can be effected by his original plan of replacing Glossu as governor of Arrakis, with Feyd-Rautha in the role of a liberating hero.

As commander of the Fremen resistance to Harkonnen occupation, Paul, despite his unparalleled military success, must prove himself by the conventional measures of Fremen manhood: for instance, by riding a sandworm. In the traditional Fremen order, Paul would have been forced to call out and kill Stilgar to succeed him as leader of Sietch Tabr, but he manages to convince his followers that such a waste is unnecessary since his claims to power as the duke extend over the whole planet, not a single community. Paul also tests himself by transforming the sacramental poison in the same manner as a Reverend Mother, something no male has ever done. During one of his military actions, Paul is reunited with Gureny Halleck, who has been living since the coup as a spice smuggler, plotting for the day he can assassinate Glossu Harkonnen.

Once it becomes clear that the Fremen are on the verge of winning their war against the Harkonnen, the Spacing Guild transports to Arrakis Emperor Shaddam IV, together with five legions of Sardaukar and military contingents from all the Great Houses of the galaxy. However, Paul has foreseen this day and developed a plan to overcome this vast military expedition and to secure his own position not only as duke but as emperor. Before his plan goes into action, however, the Sardaukar raid Sietch Tabr, kill Paul's son Leto, and take Alia captive. While Alia is being interviewed by the emperor, she kills Baron Harkonnen. Paul defeats the invading Sardaukar by using his arsenal of nuclear weapons to blow a hole in the shield wall, the mountains that surround the north pole of Arrakis. This allows a devastating desert storm to roll through the imperial encampment. This is followed by the Fremen army, riding sandworms that make short work of the imperial spacecraft and the Sardaukar they shelter. Paul takes a group of nobles captive, including the emperor and representatives of the Spacing Guild. He explains to them that if the Guild does not disperse the main elements of the invasion fleet still in orbit, and if the emperor does not abdicate in his favor (giving Paul his daughter Irulan in an official marriage that would legalize the succession), he will destroy the spice, which can be easily done by interrupting the life cycle of the sandworms. Faced with this terrorist threat that would end interstellar travel in the Imperium, Paul's adversaries must accept his conditions. The climax of the novel comes in a duel fought between Paul and Feyd-Rautha in satisfaction of the vendetta between their families. Paul's virtue easily overcomes Harkonnen treachery. Although it does not begin within the scope of the novel, the Fremen jihad across the galaxy will shortly take place because it is an imperative of human evolution.

Appendices

Four appendices contain pseudodocuments supposedly produced within the Dune universe, similar to the chapter epigraphs. They explain in a more systematic fashion material already presented in the novel concerning the ecology of Arrakis, the Bene Gesserit, and the religious history of the Imperium, and they supply brief biographies of the main characters holding ranks of nobility.

Characters

Alia Atreides

Alia is the daughter of Leto and Jessica. She was conceived only a few days before her father's death. As a result of Jessica drinking the water of life, the sacramental poison of the Fremen, while pregnant with her, Alia becomes fully self-aware while still in the womb and has an adult consciousness. She becomes known as St. Alia of the Knife because she takes revenge for her father by assassinating her grandfather, Baron Harkonnen.

Duke Leto Atreides

Duke Leto is Paul's father. The family name derives from the family that led the Greek forces in the Trojan War (perhaps because of the fulfilled prophecy concerning Agamemnon's treacherous death). Leto is aware that a member of the nobility is supposed to act in the ideal—with honor, justice, and courage—and does so to the best of his ability. His genuine virtues make him popular among the other noble houses of the Landsraad. Even the emperor, ultimately his deadly enemy, secretly wishes that Leto were his son. However, the duke's very popularity creates jealously among other houses, such as the Harkonnens, and the emperor, whose lack of a male heir makes him nervous of any potential rival. Overwhelmed by the Byzantine plots in which he finds himself enmeshed on Arrakis and disgusted by what he views as his own hypocrisy in promoting his image through propaganda, the duke finally tells Paul, "I'm morally tired. The melancholy degeneration of the Great Houses has afflicted me at last, perhaps." After his assassination by the Harkonnens, he becomes a venerated martyr in the new political and religious order instituted by Paul.

Paul Atreides

Paul is the son of Duke Leto Atreides and his concubine Lady Jessica. His birth was part of the Bene Gesserit breeding program to produce the Kwisatz Haderach, a male Bene Gesserit. However, he was intended to be born a girl who would breed with Feyd-Rautha Harkonnen and complete the program. When Jessica used her prana-bindu training to produce a son to satisfy the desires of the Duke, the birth completely upset the Bene Gesserit plans and the static system of the Imperium. Trained as a Bene Gesserit and a mentat and a user of the prophecy-inducing spice, Paul combines in himself all of the mental disciplines developed to expand human potential in place of technology. In a development completely unforeseen by the Bene Gesserit, he discovers he has the ability not only to see into the future but to shape it, realizing that small decisions of his will produce disproportionate changes in events as they unfold. His abilities are not unlimited, but he eventually chooses a path that makes him emperor and allows the fulfillment of what Herbert considers to be the primary human instinct, to indiscriminately mix pools of genetic difference. The cost, however, is the unleashing of a galaxy-wide war that will cause billions of deaths.

At the beginning of the story, Paul is a fifteen-year-old boy who must rapidly face the death of his father, his exile into a community of the desert, and the realization of his unique powers and position. Becoming a guerilla leader fighting against the Harkonnen, he must come to terms with the necessities of killing, as well as with the new experience of love with his mistress Chani. Among the Fremen, he is given the personal name Usul (meaning "base of the pillar") and the public name Muad'Dib (after the constellation of the mouse). As the plot of the novel develops, the presentation of Paul's character becomes less distinct and immediate; many of the sayings attributed to him in the epigraphs by Irulan cannot easily be reconciled with his character as portrayed in the novel. Perhaps these developments are deliberate, emphasizing Paul's movement beyond the sphere of the comprehensibly human.

Chani

Chani is the daughter of Liet-Kynes. Once Paul takes up life among the Fremen, she becomes his concubine and the heir to his mother as Reverend Mother. She also bears his son Leto II, who is killed in a Sardaukar raid. Paul praises her for her wisdom.

Count Hasimir Fenring

"A dapper and ugly little man," Count Fenring had been the imperial agent on Arrakis before the transferal of the planet to the Atreides. The closest friend of Emperor Shaddam IV, he is a "Genetic-eunuch and one of the deadliest fighters in the Imperium." His sterility was a failure of Bene Gesserit breeding. He had been intended as a candidate to become the Kwisatz Haderach. In the climax of the novel, he saves his friend Shaddam's life by refusing to duel with Paul.

Countess Margot Fenring

Countess Fenring, a Bene Gesserit, is the wife of Count Fenring. As a fellow member of the sisterhood, she leaves in the ducal residence in Arrakeen a document warning Jessica of various traps and plots prepared on Arrakis by the Harkonnens. She is later assigned by the Bene Gesserit to become pregnant by Feyd-Rautha Harkonnen so as not to lose his genetic material for their breeding program.

Gurney Halleck

Halleck is a senior officer in Duke Leto's military; he serves as fencing master to Paul. His personality possesses curious, contrary features: "a head full of songs, quotations, and flowery phrases … and the heart of an assassin when it [comes] to dealing with the Harkonnens." He survived the

Harkonnen coup and led a small remnant of Atreides soldiers who worked as spice smugglers. He eventually rejoins Paul and his Death Commandos. After Paul becomes emperor, Gurney is made Earl of Caladan.

Feyd-Rautha Rabban Harkonnen

Feyd-Rautha is the younger nephew of Baron Harkonnen. Though he has been corrupted by his uncle's influence, his genetic material is vital to the Bene Gesserit, and when it proves impossible to breed him with a daughter of Duke Leto, his line is preserved by having Countess Fenring seduce him. He is chosen by the baron not only as his successor but as a potential heir to the imperial succession. His public persona is based on his prominence as a gladiator on the Harkonnen home world of Gedei Prime. Like the ancient Roman emperor Commodus, he has won more than a thousand matches, all of which were rigged in his favor. At the climax of the novel he is anxious to resolve the feud between the Houses of Harkonnen and Atreides in a duel with Paul (a scene based on the ending of Shakespeare's *Hamlet*, complete with poisoned swords), in part because he longs to test himself in a relatively fair fight. He proves no match for Paul, who is hardened by years of actual combat experience.

Count Glossu Rabban Harkonnen

Rabban is the older nephew of Baron

Harkonnen. He was the ineffectual governor of Arrakis before the plot of the novel begins, becoming known as Beast Rabban because of his excessive cruelty. He was restored to that post after the baron regained control of the planet and given instructions to maximize revenue at all costs. This is part of the baron's plan to make his eventual replacement by his younger brother seem like a deliverance.

Baron Vladimir Harkonnen

Vladimir Harkonnen is the chief villain of *Dune*. While many names in the novel were chosen to evoke Arabic culture, the baron's is decidedly Russian, to evoke the Cold War hostility toward the Soviet Union prevalent in the early 1960s. In contrast to Duke Leto's asceticism, the baron devotes himself to every kind of depravity in pursuit of physical pleasure. One result of this is that he is immensely fat and has to support his weight with "suspensors." Also in contrast to Leto, the baron believes that people can be ruled only by manipulation and cruelty. He sets in motion the action of the novel by involving the emperor in a complicated scheme of treachery and deception that he hopes will destroy his ancestral enemies, the Atredies, and eventually maneuver his nephew Feyd-Rautha into a position to succeed the emperor. His motivation is largely simple hatred of the Atreides, of whose more legitimate and popular position he is jealous, and because "an Atreides had a Harkonnen banished for cowardice after the battle of Corrin." His family is nevertheless of great interest to the Bene Gesserit eugenics program to breed the Kwisatz Haderach. Accordingly, the Bene Gesserit lured him into fathering a child who eventually became Lady Jessica. She was later ordered to produce a daughter with Duke Leto, whose offspring from Feyd-Rautha would hopefully become the male Bene Gesserit. This makes Baron Harkonnen not only Jessica's father but the grandfather of her children, Paul and Alia. His granddaughter Alia eventually assassinates him in revenge for her father's death.

Thufir Hawat

Hawat is Duke Leto's mentat, effectively his chief of staff. He is recognized as one of the greatest mentats in the galaxy and has served the Atreides family for generations. Once he is taken captive by the Baron Harkonnen, he begins to work for him as a mentat in exchange for the possibility of taking revenge against the emperor. Remaining loyal to Paul to the last, he reveals in the final meeting between Paul and the emperor that the latter has been foolish enough to order him to assassinate his rightful lord.

Duncan Idaho

A top official in Duke Leto's military, Duncan is made ambassador to the Fremen once Leto takes control of Arrakis. During Baron Harkonnen's coup, he dies fighting Sardaukar to buy time for Paul and

Jessica's escape. He is later venerated as an important martyr of the Atreides regime.

Princess Irulan

Irulan is a Bene Gesserit and the daughter of the emperor. She plays a relatively minor role in the text of the novel. Paul must marry her to legitimize his succession as emperor. The marriage is entirely for form's sake, and she will live out her days in the fashion of a wife sent to a convent in the Middle Ages. However, she devotes the rest of her life to the production of scholarly works about Paul, and it is from these that the epigraphs at the head of each chapter are drawn.

Lady Jessica

Jessica is the concubine of Duke Leto Atreides and mother of his heir, Paul. A Bene Gesserit, she betrays her order's plan to breed the duke's daughter with Feyd-Rautha Harkonnen. Escaping to the desert Fremen with Paul, she becomes his closest adviser and mentor. She becomes a Reverend Mother through the biochemical transformation of poison, a Bene Gesserit practice that has been preserved among the Fremen. Jessica shapes Paul's life into the pattern of messianic expectation among the Fremen. This pattern of belief was in turn sown as myth among them thousands of years before by Bene Gesserit agents of the Missonaria Protectiva so that it could be exploited by any future Bene Gesserit marooned among the Fremen.

Muad'Dib

See Paul Atreides

Pardot Liet-Kynes

Pardot Liet-Kynes is the Imperial Planetologist on Arrakis. As an imperial official, he holds the position of Judge of the Change for the transition of power between the Harkonnens and Atreides. He inherited his position as planetologist from his father, also named Pardot. The elder planetologist had convinced the Fremen that by following his plan they could convert Arrakis into a paradise with open water and large tracts of vegetation. In deference to this plan, he became their de facto leader, using them as a work force to plant and protect plants in the southern hemisphere. He married a Fremen woman, and his son also has the Fremen name, Liet. During the coup, Liet-Kynes saves Paul and Jessica by sending them to the Fremen of the deep desert, but he dies while trying to escape the Sardaukar

Gaius Helen Mohaim

She is a Bene Gesserit Reverend Mother and the emperor's truthsayer. She has had the mind-expanding experience of consciously using her body's biochemistry to neutralize the water of life poison, the highest level of Bene Gesserit training. As a result, she has a heightened awareness of subtle cues in her perceptual field, and can easily tell whether someone speaking to her is lying or not. She makes a special trip to Caladan to test Paul with the gom jabr. Ordered to evaluate Paul to see whether he is the Kwisatz Haderach, she unconsciously blinds herself to the evidence. She is present in the final audience scene with Paul, principally as the representative of the Bene Gesserit order, so that Paul can gloat to her over his complete destruction of their breeding scheme.

Emperor Shadam IV

Shadam is the emperor of the galactic Imperium. He sets the plot of *Dune* in motion by conspiring with the Harkonnens to destroy the Atreides family, something he feels is a political necessity because they have trained their own military to a standard equivalent to his Sardaukar corps, upsetting the balance between emperor and nobles. Nevertheless, he idealizes Duke Leto more than anyone else, and his daughter Irulan perceives that her father wishes the duke were his son. When he is utterly defeated, Paul offers him the face-saving way out of accepting Paul as heir through marriage to Princess Irulan. Irulan prevents her father from rejecting Paul's mercy by using the Bene Gesserit trick of appealing to his deepest unconscious wishes at a moment of crisis, telling him of Paul, "But here's a man fit to be your son."

Stilgar

Stilgar is the leader of the Sietch Tabr. (This

community is probably named after Mt. Tabor, the hill outside Jerusalem where tradition says the Transfiguration of Christ took place, and an important name in medieval messianic movements in Central Europe.) He originally led the Fremen embassy to Duke Leto and created a stir with the duke's bodyguard by spitting at his feet, but this was a sign of desert honor rather than a challenge. He becomes Paul's protector among the Fremen after the Harkonnen coup. Although Stilgar becomes Paul's chief lieutenant during the guerilla war against the Harkonnen and governor of Arakkis after Paul becomes emperor, Paul considers that he is inherently diminished to something less than human to the same degree Paul himself must play the role of the more than human: "Paul saw how Stilgar has been transformed from the Fremen nain to a *creature* of the Lisan al-Gaib, a receptacle for awe and obedience. It was a lessening of the man."

Usul

See Paul Atreides

Piter De Vries

De Vries is the sadistic mentat of the Baron Harkonnen. Before being killed in Duke Leto's final attempt to assassinate the baron, De Vries invents a poison that will remain in the body indefinitely with no effect so long as an antidote is regularly administered. This is later used by the baron to control Thufir Hawat.

Wellington Yueh

Yueh is the personal physician of Duke Leto. He was a Suk Doctor, meaning he has undergone psychological conditioning to make it impossible for him to betray his master, an important consideration among nobles who live in constant dread of assassination. His betrayal of the duke makes the swift advance of the baron's coup possible. The baron believes he has broken Yueh's conditioning by torturing his wife and securing his treachery in exchange for stopping the torture and the promise returning her to him. However, the actual factor involved was Yueh's hope for revenge against the baron, which he nearly achieves by implanting a false tooth filled with poison gas into Duke Leto's mouth, to kill the baron as he gloats over him in triumph. However, this plan does not ultimately work.

Themes

Religion

The main theme of *Dune* is the disastrous effect that messianic religious belief can have on human society. Herbert's original inspiration was the messianic cult of personality that was attached to Adolf Hitler, who exploited the power it gave him to start World War II and the Holocaust. Herbert treats this through fiction in the messianic role Paul plays for the Fremen and the eugenics program of the Bene Gesserit, as well as in the anti-eugenic disaster unleashed across the galaxy by the Fremen.

Topics for Further Study

- Draw some sketches of your favorite

characters from *Dune*. Then, compare them to the way the characters were drawn in the 1984 *Dune* comic book (*Marvel Super Special 36*) by Bill Sienkiewicz. Report to your class on the differing artistic approaches.

- George Lucas, the writer and director of the *Star Wars* movies, does not deny that much of the fictional world and plot of that series was derived from *Dune*. View one or more of Lucas's films and give a PowerPoint presentation explaining some items that are similar to material in *Dune*.
- Robert Heinlein's 1961 novel *Stranger in a Strange Land* arguably did as much to change the nature of the science fiction genre as *Dune*. The novels are very different in form, style, and language, but they treat many of the same themes. Write a review comparing and contrasting the two books.
- Religion plays an important, if unorthodox, role in *Dune*. Present an oral report to your class on some similarities between the religions presented in Dune and the real-world faiths of Christianity and Islam.

- Choose one of the short stories from *The Year's Best "Science Fiction" and Fantasy for Teens: First Annual Collection*, edited by Jane Yolen and Patrick Nielsen Hayden (2005). Look for comparisons to *Dune* in terms of theme and style. Write an essay that sums up your findings.

Technology and Human Development

The fantastic advance of technology has always been a common theme of science fiction. There are certainly some instances of superscience in *Dune*, but Herbert's treatment of such marvels stands far apart from most science fiction. Many of the technological ideas used in *Dune* in 1965 have already been surpassed by modern science. For instance, the ornithopters used as aircraft on Arrakis underperform modern helicopters and jets. In general, the level of technology in *Dune* is relatively primitive; the water reprocessing stillsuits used by the Fremen have a "green" rather than a high-tech feel. Even items such as the interstellar travel used by the Spacing Guild and the shields used as personal protection by soldiers function rather strangely in the book. They can hardly be said to be technological marvels since they have no conceivable basis in physics and so are more nearly devices of fantasy than of scientific extrapolation.

In fact, Herbert uses the ships and navigators of the Spacing Guild to avoid having to deal realistically with the effect of space travel on society. The characters might as well be magically transported from Caladan to Arrakis so that they can get on with the action. The shields work similarly: they make firearms and energy weapons such as lasers practically useless, so soldiers have reverted to fighting with swords, whose relatively slow movements can penetrate the shields. Herbert purposefully ignores technological advancement to emphasize the development of purely human potential. The initial objection to the use of firearms in war at the end of the Middle Ages was that a knight who had trained at arms for ten years could be killed on the battlefield by a peasant with a musket who had trained for ten minutes. Herbert wanted to reverse that development and imagine to what heights and extremes the training of human abilities could reach. The exploration of technological advancement is rejected in favor of the exploration of human advancement. The abandonment of computers during the Butlerian Jihad "forced *human* minds to develop. Schools were started to train *human* talents." This is manifested in the prophetic abilities of the Spacing Guild navigators, in the seemingly magical powers of perception and self-control perfected by the Bene Gesserit, and in the computing ability of the mentats. All of these qualities are combined in Paul, who as the Kwisatz Haderach of the Bene Gesserit and the messiah of the Fremen represents a new level of human evolution and potential.

Eugenics

Inasmuch as the historical phenomena of the rapid rise to power and striking initial success of Adolph Hitler were among Herbert's inspirations, it is not surprising that eugenics is an important theme of *Dune*. Eugenics (literally "wellborn") is the effort to breed human beings like domestic animals to achieve some apparently desirable new trait or to shift the composition of a population. It involves controlling which human beings may breed with others or even the sterilization or culling (i.e., murder) of supposedly undesirable specimens. It is one of the most outrageous violations of human rights imaginable. There are nevertheless two important eugenics programs in the Dune universe.

The civilization depicted in *Dune* has endured for over ten thousand years; during that time, the imperial family has controlled Salusa Secundus, a planet whose environment is extremely hostile to human life. The planet was originally used as a prison, and the emperors relied on the environmental conditions there to select for "tough, strong, ferocious men" who were naturally suited for warfare. This eventually created the Sardaukar guard of the emperor, the greatest soldiers in the empire. Or rather, the second greatest, since the even more extreme conditions on Arrakis produced the Fremen, who were correspondingly better fighters, only in this case by an entirely natural evolution. "God created Arrakis to train the faithful" is a Fremen saying. The fact that human intentions to imitate or control nature are doomed to ultimate failure is an important point of the novel: artificial breeding cannot outdo evolution. Although Herbert intended the Sardaukar as a thought experiment to play out something like the Nazi eugenics program on a larger scale (it is clear that the Sardaukar are modeled after the Nazi SS), it is quite fantastic. In fact, the human cultures of the most extreme desert environments, the Bushmen of the Kalahari and the Australian Aborigines, depend for survival on cooperation and altruism, with the result that they are remarkably unwarlike.

The primary purpose of the Bene Gesserit Sisterhood was to breed a man who could look into some part of the human consciousness that they, as women, were blind to (the part that takes and is inherently male, as Paul later describes it). This was the Kwisatz Haderach (Shortening of the Way), whom they hoped could see where the Reverend Mothers could not. To this end, the Bene Gesserit established a social position for themselves wherein most young aristocratic women joined the Bene Gesserit, and the Bene Gesserit supplied wives and concubines to the aristocrats of the empire. By keeping track of the often secret paternity of children born to these unions and carefully interbreeding the various families, they control the genetic destiny of the whole imperial aristocracy and manipulate the nobility for the purposes of their covert eugenics program. Their final plan is to produce the Kwisatz Haderach by breeding the daughter of Duke Leto and Jessica (secretly the daughter of Baron Harkonnen) with the baron's nephew Feyd-Rautha. However, out of her love for

Leto, Jessica instead bears a boy, Paul. He upsets all of the Bene Gesserit plans by becoming the Kwisatz Haderach (and much else besides) entirely outside of their control. Paul eventually realizes that his destiny, which the Bene Gesserit have been breeding for without realizing it, is to unleash a devastating war across the galaxy. This war, countering every effort at eugenics, will indiscriminately mix the genetic material of all human populations: "They were all caught up in the need for their race to renew its scattered inheritance, to cross and mingle and infuse their bloodlines in a great new pooling of genes." Herbert views eugenics as a system that is ultimately self-defeating, aside from its moral repugnance, because it is contrary to a nature that will not be denied. Herbert told his biographer Timothy O'Reilly, "I can state it for you very straightly: human beings are not through evolving. And if we are going to survive as a species, we're going to have to do things that allow us to keep on evolving."

Ecology

In the 1960s, it was becoming increasingly apparent that modern industrial society was transforming, even damaging, the natural world, as population increased dramatically and industrial processes were carried out on ever larger scales, using irreplaceable resources and generating increasing amounts of dangerous waste. *Dune* was of great interest to the nascent environmental movement because, in the Fremen's attempt to restore open water and green areas to Arrakis, it offered a model of ecological repair.

Style

Science Fiction

Science fiction and the closely allied genre of fantasy (*Dune* is often said to have elements of both) is difficult to define. A simple definition based on elements common in the genre, such as space travel, stories set in the future, and so on, or even a more sophisticated attempt at definition such as a 'literature of ideas,' is not sufficient, since many books contain those elements but are not science fiction. Works by authors such as Doris Lessing, Anthony Burgess, or Margaret Atwood meet those simple criteria and yet they have never been considered science fiction by critics, and the authors themselves more or less vociferously deny that their works are science fiction. A historical definition of the genre is more useful (leaving aside the works of authors such as H. G. Wells or Jules Verne, which are best seen as precursors of the purely genre development). Science fiction developed in the 1920s in the United States along with a series of pulp (mass-marketed) journals that capitalized on the increasing public perception of the transformation being effected in society by the hastening pace of technological change (such as radio and the dispersion of the automobile). The creator of the science fiction magazines was Hugo Gernsback, who had long published journals devoted to amateur radio enthusiasts. Gernsback began publishing *Amazing Stories* in 1926; this and similar magazines were called "pulps" after the cheap paper stock on which they were printed. The formula of the science fiction genre was established by John W. Campbell, who from 1938 to 1971 edited *Astounding Science Fiction.* The genre originally consisted of relatively simplistic stories whose interest was generated by fantastically advanced technology (indistinguishable from magic as Arthur C. Clarke said) such as robots with intelligence and feelings comparable to human beings or interstellar space flight. The primary audience for these magazines in the 1920s to the 1950s consisted of teenage boys, and many of science fiction's themes of adventure, warfare, and heroism—fantasies of power—catered to that audience. Most decisively, there was only a superficial contact between the language and style of science fiction and the wider world of literature as a whole. It was the isolation of a small, self-contained world of science fiction authors (such as E. E. Smith, Robert Heinlein, and Isaac Asimov) and readers (fans) that created science fiction as a genre, while at the same time other authors, such as Aldous Huxley, George Orwell, and William Golding, were treating very similar themes in writing intended for a more general audience. Herbert's work, before and after *Dune*, corresponds to the profile of genre science fiction, as noted by critic David Miller: "Most of Herbert's novels seem designed to be read once; hence story lines are clear, there is little parallel action, genre markers are unequivocal, and proleptic [anticipatory] clues are relatively obvious." *Dune*, however, broke out of this generic mold in a way that had never been seen before in science fiction. While Dune's characters remain for the most part stereotypes, Herbert was successful in making the plot and its meaning arise from the characters, and especially from the character of the narrative world he created, thus introducing new levels of literary sophistication while staying within the genre. This made it possible to do real literary work in the science fiction genre, and while science fiction still maintains its distance from other literature and still produces a great deal of material that follows the old pulp formulas, it was forever transformed by the presence of *Dune* within it.

Series Fiction

It is a peculiarity of science fiction publishing that a popular novel will often initiate a series of sequels (by the same author or others). The resulting series of books may not all contain the same characters or discuss the same themes, but they will take place in the same "universe." That is, the books will all share the same premise about the development of future history and technology, take place in the same alternative universe, or share other essential features of the original's setting. This trend exists largely because of the economic realities of publishing. It is easier to sell readers books that they already have some familiarity with, and writers frequently have extensive background notes compiled for the original novel that can be exploited in this way. Perhaps the prototype for this kind of publishing is L. Frank Baum's *The Wonderful Wizard of Oz*, to which Baum wrote thirteen sequels and, after his death, other writers an additional twenty-six. The sequels are aimed at a specific fan base who read the original book and not at new readers. The pattern has been repeated endlessly in science fiction publishing (and to a lesser degree in mystery novels and other genres). Fans pride themselves on their knowledge of the "canon" of particular series, and a technical literature of encyclopedias and dictionaries relating to a series is often produced as well (though usually not by the writer or writers of the series). Herbert resisted this trend in some respects in that he introduced radically new concepts in his sequels, ideas that often undercut or reinterpreted material in the original novel and that many of his readers found distressing, but that he had deemed integral to the overall story from the original inception of the project. In *Dune*, Herbert included several appendices of reference material and a glossary of terms used in the languages he fabricated for *Dune*. He also encouraged his colleague Willis McNelly to create additional fabricated historical documents in *The Dune Encyclopedia*, although he eventually repudiated the new fictional material in this work as "noncanonical." However, Herbert finally became trapped in a situation in which he had to write more Dune sequels because sales and therefore publishers' advances were much larger for books in the Dune series than for anything else he could write. His son, Brian Herbert, has found himself in the same position; he has written eleven additional sequels and announced plans to produce about one novel a year indefinitely. Each sequel goes onto the *New York Times* best-seller list, while his original books enjoy lesser popularity.

Compare & Contrast

- **1960s:** Computer technology is primitive and has little direct impact on people's lives; the absence of computers in *Dune* is not very noticeable.

  Today: A majority of people use a computer and the Internet every day for work and pleasure; the absence of computers in *Dune* is striking.

- **1960s:** The United States is committed to a rapidly escalating and ultimately unsuccessful guerilla war in the rain forests of Vietnam.

  Today: U.S. forces are fighting in Iraq and Afghanistan, areas where the climate and culture provide striking parallels to the guerilla war in *Dune* and its ideological and geographical setting.

- **1960s:** Although the space race is widely followed in popular media, it is something to be watched almost as a drama on television rather than a concrete reality in people's lives.

Today: The use of space is widespread and completely integrated into mainstream culture through the use of weather prediction satellites, telecommunications, global positioning systems, and many other areas. These space-based technologies are ubiquitous and are sometimes taken for granted.

Historical Context

General Semantics

In the 1930s, the Polish American engineer Alfred Korzybski developed the discipline of general semantics (not to be confused with ordinary semantics, the study of the meaning of words) and founded a school for instruction in his system. General semantics holds that language is a metaphorical abstraction that actually separates the human mind from objects of thought. He wished to use mathematics as a model for a new way of thinking that would suspend ordinary semantic categories (words) and allow the mind to deal directly with reality. For instance, a rose is not the word *rose*. Korzybski believed that a tremendous advance in understanding could be achieved through comprehending the thing itself rather than by using the symbolic value of its name as an intermediary. Herbert was deeply influenced by Korzybski's thought. In fact he ghostwrote a syndicated newspaper column on the subject for U.S. Senator S. I. Hayakawa. Herbert's biographer Timothy O'Reilly finds that "much of the Bene Gesserit technology of consciousness is based on the insights of general semantics." The same is true of mentat training. Whereas mentat identify themselves with the flow of the process of any phenomenon that comes under study, Bene Gesserit focus on controlling perception. They use conscious intent to control what is otherwise determined unconsciously, to truly perceive what is before them instead of filtering it through memory and other mental processes that normally suppress most possible perceptions (and of which language is only the most superficial, in Herbert's exaggeration of general semantics). By extending this practice they can control autonomic functions, such as heat rhythm and the ability to metabolize chemical substances in the body, and achieve a subtlety of perception that makes them human lie detectors (an idea that fascinated Herbert) through their perception of changes in expression and biological function of the speaker. One of the most interesting things for Herbert, though, is when a system fails to operate correctly. An example of this is Jessica not realizing that she and Paul are descended from Baron Harkonnen. Despite the telltale physical similarities, she never suspects her ancestry until Paul reveals it to her. It is not that she cannot see the resemblance—indeed, she obviously can—but she refuses to do so because it is contrary to her preconceived ideas.

Systematics

Systematics, or system thinking, is an approach to problem solving derived from mathematics and engineering. It treats any problem as part of a larger system and considers the possible effects throughout the system from changing one element of it, as well as the possibility of effecting system-wide change by making small changes in one or a few system components. In the course of his work as a journalist, Herbert became fascinated with an example of what he considered a systematic approach to problem solving, namely the stabilization of sand dunes that constantly threatened to engulf the town of Florence, Oregon. Rather than a massive public works project involving hauling away millions of tons of sand (which would not have solved the problem of the natural forces that formed the dunes to begin with), the dunes were stabilized by a very small-scale planting of specific plant species. This was one of the most important sources for his conception of *Dune*, which essentially scales the process up to transforming a whole planet, as Herbert explains in detail in the first appendix to the novel. Another influence of systematics in *Dune* is seen in the epigraphs from Irulan's scholarly works at the beginning of each chapter. By revealing the "future," that is, key points of the plot, they act like the connective arrows on a flow chart, showing how the various parts of the plot are to be connected. Understanding, rather than surprise, is Herbert's aim. The same applies to Paul's visions of the future. He does not see specific unalterable events that must come to pass. Rather, he sees "a spectrum of possibilities ... from the most probable to the most improbable." That much is actually no different than anyone else trying to estimate probable outcomes, but there is more to Paul's vision: "*I have another kind of sight. I see another kind of terrain: the available paths.*" In other words, Paul sees the future as a system and can see the (possibly large) outcome of small changes that occur based on his decisions. In other words, he does not so much see the future as how to shape the future he wants through systems analysis.

The characters in Dune are for the most part clearly defined stereotypes. This is not a result of lack of skill on the author's part but rather of Herbert's interest in systematics. If the characters are in the familiar cookie-cutter shapes of the 'good nobleman,' the 'decadent monster,' the 'gruff but loveable loyal old soldier,' the 'peasant girl who becomes a princess,' and even the 'messiah,' then Herbert can build his story in the same fashion as assembling the pieces of a jigsaw into an organized pattern, all interconnected with each other like the boxes on a flow chart, rather than developing the chaotic plot that might arise from more fully developed characters.

Critical Overview

Brian Aldiss's *Billion Year Spree* is the seminal work of genre science fiction criticism. Writing only six years after the publication of *Dune*, Aldiss already stresses that Herbert's novel breaks out of the science fiction mold perfected in the 1930s by author and editor John W. Campbell:

> Its readers can indulge in a fantasy life of power and savour a strange religion. But there is more than that to *Dune*.... Although Campbellian science fiction is still present, so, too, is an attention to sensuous detail which is the antithesis of Campbell.

Aldiss realizes the novel has depths that repay careful reading, but also judges its ecological themes to be trendy.

One of the earliest academic assessments of *Dune* came in David Miller's critical monograph on *Frank Herbert*. In Miller's view, the main theme of all of Herbert's work, especially of his greatest novel, is the necessity for balance:

> 1.) If man does not achieve a balance within himself and with his environment, existence is merely a version of chaos. 2.) If man freezes an achieved balance, decadence sets in and life yields to entropy. Thus the

> problems to be solved by Herbert's characters require that chaos be organized and stasis disturbed. The desideratum is dynamic homeostasis.

This nicely captures Herbert's interest in systematics. One of the most important sources of information about Herbert's own views of *Dune* and the process of its composition is Timothy O'Reilly's 1981 biography, *Frank Herbert*. O'Reilly's discussion is based on extensive interviews with Herbert. Peter Minowitz, writing in *Political Science Fiction*, compares the actual political deeds of the Atreides and Harkonnens and finds that they are not so different as the novel's appeal to a stark dichotomy of good and evil might suggest, but that rather both sides follow Machiavelli's statements regarding the use of power.

A theme of recent criticism has been to view *Dune* as, far from radical, old-fashioned. Michael R. Collings's contribution to *Aspects of Fantasy* speculates that while the poetic epic form died out in English after reaching its apex with John Milton, much of the essential content might survive in the modern form of the novel. Citing *The Lord of the Rings* as an obvious example and suggesting that *Dune* is another, he demonstrates that the surface narrative of Herbert's novel is composed of traditional epic themes of valor, camaraderie, hierarchy, and the drawing-out of strong emotion. Julia List, in her article "Call Me a Protestant," in the 2009 issue of *Science Fiction Studies*, points out that although Herbert rejects the radical messianism depicted in *Dune* as destructive, he embraces nevertheless the values of 1960s elite mainline American Protestantism without examination to "serve as a secular cultural code that unites the elite." Adam Charles Roberts, in his *Science Fiction*, views Herbert's presentation of a traditional male ideology of power through royal lineage, messianism, warfare, and aggression as an implicit criticism of such power structures.

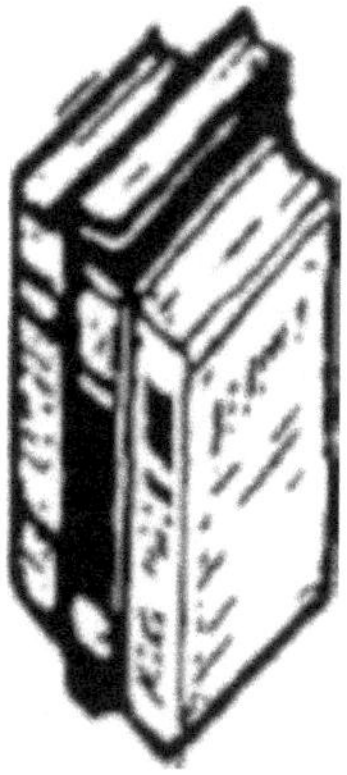

What Do I Read Next?

- Much of the culture and religion of *Dune* is derived from Arab culture and Islam. An overview of this background for younger readers is provided by Mitchell Young's 2005 compilation *Religions and Religious Movements: Islam.*
- *The Saviour God: Comparative Studies in the Concept of Salvation*

Presented to Edwin Oliver Kames, edited by S. G. F. Brandon and published in 1963, provides a cross-cultural survey of messianic figures, representing the state of scholarship on the question at the time Herbert wrote *Dune*.

- In 1969, Herbert published his first sequel to *Dune*, *Dune Messiah*, which had been planned as a continuation of the original novel.
- In 1976, Herbert completed the *Dune* trilogy with *Children of Dune*. Although this completed his original concept, the popularity of the series led him to write several more *Dune* novels.
- The official *Dune* Web site (http://www.dunenovels.com) hosts a Web log written by Brian Herbert and Kevin J. Anderson, the authors of the continuing "Dune" series, along with a discussion forum and a variety of *Dune* resource materials.
- *The Best of John W. Campbell*, published in 1976, collects the most important work by arguably the most important and influential writer in traditional science fiction in the era before Herbert's *Dune*.

Sources

Aldiss, Brian W., *Billion Year Spree: The True History of Science Fiction*, Doubleday, 1973, pp. 274-76.

Checkland, Peter, *Systems Thinking, Systems Practice*, Wiley, 1981.

Collings, Michael R., "The Epic of *Dune*: Epic Traditions in Modern Science Fiction," in *Aspects of Fantasy: Selected Essays from the Second International Conference on the Fantastic in Literature and Film*, edited by William Coyle, Greenwood Press, 1986, pp. 131-39.

Herbert, Brian, *Dreamer of Dune: The Biography of Frank Herbert*, Tor, 2003.

Herbert, Frank, *Dune: Fortieth Anniversary Edition*, Ace Books, 2005.

———, "Dune Genesis," in *Omni* July 1980, pp. 72-75.

Killingsworth, M. Jimmie, and Jacqueline S. Palmer, "Silent Spring and Science Fiction: An Essay in the History and Rhetoric of Narrative," in *And No Birds Sing: Rhetorical Analyses of Rachel Carson's Silent Spring*, edited by Craig Waddell, University of Illinois at Carbondale Press, 2000, pp. 174-204.

List, Julia, "'Call Me a Protestant': Liberal Christianity, Individualism, and the Messiah in

Stranger in a Strange Land, *Dune*, and *Lord of Light*," in *Science Fiction Studies*, Vol. 36, No. 1, 2009, pp. 21-47.

McNelly, Willis, E., *The Dune Encyclopedia*, Ace Books, 1984.

Miller, David M., *Frank Herbert*, Starmount House, 1980, pp. 15-26.

Minowitz, Peter, "Prince versus Prophet: Machiavellianism in Frank Herbert's *Dune* Epic," in *Political Science Fiction*, edited by Donald M. Hassler and Clyde Wilcox, University of South Carolina Press, 1997, pp. 124-47.

O'Reilly, Timothy, *Frank Herbert*, Frederick Ungar, 1981, pp. 39, 59, 166.

Roberts, Adam Charles, *Science Fiction*, Routledge, 2000, pp. 36-46.

Stratton, Susan, "The Messiah and the Greens: The Shape of Environmental Action in *Dune* and *Pacific Edge*," in *Extrapolation*, Vol. 42, 2001, pp. 303-18.

Further Reading

Grazier, Kevin Robert, *The Science of Dune*, BenBella Books, 2007.

In this book, physicist Kevin Robert Grazier explores possible real-world scientific explanations for some of the technology and human transformations envisioned by Herbert.

Khazanov, Anatoly Michailovich, *Nomads and the Outside World*, translated by Julia Cookenden, 2nd ed., University of Wisconsin Press, 1994.

Khazanov presents an illuminating study of the nomadic desert societies that were part of Herbert's inspiration for the Fremen in *Dune*.

O'Reilly, Tim, ed., *The Maker of Dune: Insights of a Master of Science Fiction*, Berkley Books, 1987.

Shortly after Herbert's death, O'Reilly edited this collection of nonfiction essays by the author of *Dune*.

Palumbo, Donald E., *Chaos Theory, Asimov's Foundations and Robots, and Herbert's Dune: The Fractal Aesthetic of Epic Science Fiction*, Contributions to the Study of Science Fiction and Fantasy 100, Greenwood Press, 2002.

Palumbo analyzes *Dune* in contrast to Asimov's Foundation series and in light of the recent popularity of chaos theory.

Lightning Source UK Ltd.
Milton Keynes UK
UKHW021400200421
382307UK00008B/1764

9 781375 400862